NO LONGE[R]
SEATTLE

COLUMBIA BRANCH
RECEIVED
AUG 26 2010

D0578606

ELIZABETH WARREN

NEVERTHELESS, SHE PERSISTED

text by **SUSAN WOOD**   pictures by **SARAH GREEN**

Abrams Books for Young Readers · **NEW YORK**

It's no surprise that Elizabeth Warren would grow up to be a fighter. A fighter for families. A fighter for those struggling to be heard. A fighter for those who need help. When Elizabeth was little, she watched her parents fight to keep her family's home. When she was a teen, she learned to fight with her words to be heard. And as a woman, she became a tireless fighter for what's fair.

  She insisted.
  She resisted.
  She persisted.
  Elizabeth's been fighting all her life.

It all started at home. When Elizabeth's mother decided her daughter would get a good education, Elizabeth's parents fought to make that happen, scraping together enough money to buy a house near the best schools in Oklahoma City. The home's wiring sparked and the plaster fell, but her daddy was handy. And there was a big yard where Mother grew irises and roses when she wasn't cooking, cleaning, and taking care of the family.

Daddy had a job selling carpet, and he bought a used car for Mother. Elizabeth loved that secondhand station wagon—its glowing color, fake leather seats, and whirring air-conditioning. The family wasn't rich, but they weren't poor either. They were middle class. Like many other families across America, they were getting by.

When Elizabeth was twelve, Daddy had a heart attack. After he came home from the hospital, he wasn't allowed to do much, not even work, because it might hurt his heart. One day, Mother picked Elizabeth up from school in Daddy's clunky old car. *Where's our glowing station wagon?* Elizabeth wondered. The family couldn't pay for the station wagon anymore, Mother told her quietly. They'd had to give it back.

So Daddy drove Elizabeth to school in his tired, rusty car, dropping her off a few blocks away so no one would see. Now Elizabeth noticed the differences between her classmates and herself—and she felt like she didn't quite fit in. The other kids wore nicer clothes. They lived in bigger houses. Elizabeth wondered if that was fair. After all, bad luck could happen to anybody, even to a hardworking family like hers.

One day Elizabeth found Mother in the dress she wore only for graduations and funerals. Her eyes were red and puffy. Elizabeth was confused. Did someone die? No, Mother explained, she was headed to a job interview at the department store. *Other kids' moms don't work,* Elizabeth thought. *Why should Mother?*

Truth hit Elizabeth like an Oklahoma twister. Her middle-class family was no longer getting by. They were poor, on the edge of losing everything, even their house.

But Mother wasn't giving in.

She was fighting the best way she knew how—by finding a job.

Mother landed the position answering phones at the department store. Daddy eventually found a new job cleaning up around an apartment building. And Elizabeth babysat, waitressed in her aunt's restaurant, and sewed dresses for money to help out the struggling family . . . all while doing so well in her schoolwork that she was able to skip a grade.

In high school, scrawny Elizabeth didn't play a sport or sing in the chorus.
Her talent, she learned when she joined the debate team, was fighting—
not with her fists, but with her words. At that time, mostly boys debated.
Standing up and speaking out—that wasn't for girls. Girls were expected to
be quiet, to be nice, to keep their views to themselves and study cooking and
housekeeping in home economics classes.

On the debate team, Elizabeth tackled hard topics and researched things she didn't know. She used facts and logic to craft thoughtful arguments, then challenged her opponents . . . and she won! As she debated her way to state champion, she learned about never giving up—about getting battered, but not beaten. Using her words, Elizabeth could be seen, she could be heard, and she could fight for herself.

Elizabeth dreamed of going to college, but she knew her family wouldn't be able to pay for it.

But Elizabeth stayed determined.

She figured out how to use her fine debate skills to win herself a scholarship.

Two years into college, Elizabeth's high-school sweetheart from debate team, Jim Warren, asked her to marry him. She said yes. Elizabeth left school, but she had a plan—she enrolled at a college in their new hometown of Houston, Texas. Elizabeth graduated—the first in her family to do so—and became a teacher for kids with special needs. But when Elizabeth and Jim had a baby, Amelia, the school didn't ask her back.

SCHOLARSHIP
AWARDED
TO
ELIZABETH

Teacher's Certificate

ELIZABETH WARREN

For a while, Elizabeth was happy making a home for her young family in New Jersey, where they now lived. But she wanted to do even more. So she went back to school—this time to become a lawyer. She had a hunch she'd like law school, particularly all the debating. She was right! Elizabeth liked the idea that maybe she could argue her way to a better world.

HARVARD LAW

After graduation, Elizabeth had trouble finding a job as a lawyer. And now she was the mother of two children; she and Jim had welcomed baby Alex into their family.

But Elizabeth didn't let that stop her.

She had a sign painted up, ELIZABETH WARREN, ATTORNEY AT LAW, and hung it by her front door. She worked right from her living room. Now, as a lawyer, Elizabeth used her words to fight for people who needed her help.

Soon universities hired Elizabeth to teach law classes. Her specialty? Laws about people who scraped together money to pay their bills but still couldn't make ends meet. Elizabeth remembered how it felt not having enough money, afraid that what you did have—your favorite glowing car, your house with the big yard—could be taken away.

PLATO
ETHICS

HOUSING
BUBBLES

Elizabeth wondered why more and more middle-class families weren't getting by anymore while the rich just seemed to get richer. So she did a lot of research. She learned that most middle-class folks weren't going broke because they bought too much stuff. Instead, they were having a hard time largely because laws had become lopsided, in favor of big banks, businesses, and people who already had a lot of money. Elizabeth didn't think that was fair.

Elizabeth remembered how hard it was for Mother and Daddy, and it made her want to stand up and speak out, to question the way things were, and to fight for how they should be. Now, as a law professor, Elizabeth used her words to fight for all those families who weren't getting by.

When a United States Senate seat opened up in Massachusetts, where Elizabeth now lived, some suggested that she would be the perfect person to fill it. Elizabeth had never run for political office before; she thought of herself as a teacher. Plus, Massachusetts had never elected a woman senator. Still, there was so much at stake, Elizabeth believed. She'd spent years fighting for families trying to get by, and there was more work to do. What if banks and politicians got richer and more powerful while middle-class folks were left with less and had to struggle even harder? Elizabeth didn't think that was fair.

Elizabeth wondered if she could make a difference by becoming a senator. To help her decide, Elizabeth met with people in living rooms and backyards all over Massachusetts. She listened to their concerns and shared what she had discovered about why ordinary people were struggling so much. At one meeting, a woman told Elizabeth that she'd walked two miles to get there because she'd lost her job and her car and she didn't know if she'd ever find a job again. "I'm running out of hope," the woman said. "I want you to fight for me."

Elizabeth made up her mind right then and there.
"Yes," she declared. "I'll fight."

Elizabeth hit the campaign trail. In speeches and interviews and at public meetings across the state, she promised to fight to make sure everyone had an equal chance to get ahead. Campaigning wasn't easy.

But Elizabeth never gave up.

She got battered, but not beaten . . . and she won! Now, as a senator, Elizabeth was fighting for families, for workers, for students and the elderly, for the whole middle class.

One duty of a senator is to consider the people that a newly elected president wants to put in certain jobs. When a new president suggested another senator for the government's top lawyer position, a man Elizabeth felt strongly wasn't a good fit, she stood up and spoke out. She tried to share a letter that Coretta Scott King, the widow of civil rights leader Martin Luther King Jr., had written criticizing the senator. As Elizabeth read aloud in the Senate chamber, she was interrupted. She was warned of a rarely used rule about speaking against a fellow senator. Elizabeth didn't think that was fair.

So Elizabeth kept at it.

As she continued to speak out, she was interrupted again and told to sit down. Another senator silenced her, telling the Senate, "She was warned. She was given an explanation. Nevertheless, she persisted."

But Elizabeth didn't back down.

She persisted indeed.

Although she wasn't allowed to speak further inside the Senate chamber, she could still say what she needed to outside of it. So Elizabeth read Mrs. King's letter—every last word—outside the Senate doors, where her speech was broadcast live and seen by millions. "Nevertheless, she persisted" became a rallying cry for all people who've ever been told to be quiet, to be nice, to keep their thoughts and views to themselves.

Today Elizabeth Warren remains a fighter. Fighting for middle-class families. Fighting for fair and equal treatment for everyone. Fighting for those who need help. It isn't always easy.

But she never gives up.

On her journey from schoolgirl to senator, she's been battered, but not beaten.

She's insisted.

She's resisted.

And she's always, *always* persisted.

Warren Elected Senator

AUTHOR'S NOTE

Elizabeth was born on June 22, 1949, in Oklahoma City, Oklahoma, the youngest child and only daughter of Donald and Pauline Herring. Her three older brothers were all grown-up and on their own by the time Elizabeth entered high school.

Elizabeth has described her family after her father's heart attack as living on "the ragged edge of the middle class . . . kind of hanging on at the edges by our fingernails." That firsthand experience with money trouble—how it can strain a family's sense of security and belonging—is what led her to fight for middle-class families across the country.

As a law professor, Elizabeth became an expert on bankruptcy. That's the legal term for when a person can't pay their bills and their possessions are taken away as payment instead. Elizabeth remembered all too well how it felt to fret about that. In her research, she learned that middle-class families were having a hard time because fair-banking rules had been stripped away over the years. For example, regulations that made it illegal for banks to lend money at extraordinarily high interest rates were eliminated in 1978, and a 1996 court ruling allowed many banks to start charging sky-high fees to use credit cards as well. To make matters worse, prices for things like health care, housing, and education had gone up while the amount of money people made from their jobs had stayed the same. Middle-class families now had to pay more for their most basic needs. One surprise event—like losing a job or having a medical emergency, like a heart attack—could put a family in serious financial danger.

In 1995, Elizabeth was asked to advise the National Bankruptcy Review Commission, a special committee studying banking laws that hurt struggling families. She spent most of the next decade in Washington, DC, sharing her expert opinions before Congress.

Meanwhile, some banks started giving home loans to people who clearly couldn't afford to pay for them. This doesn't sound like good business, but there weren't rules to stop the banks. When homeowners couldn't make their loan payments, many banks failed. Because the banks failed, people lost their homes and jobs. To fix the damage, the government decided to loan money to the banks to get them operating again, and the US Senate asked Elizabeth to oversee the bailout. In 2008, she was appointed leader of the Congressional Oversight Panel for the Troubled Asset Relief Program.

Elizabeth had long worried about how big, powerful banks always seemed to be taking advantage of middle-class families and how the government just seemed to let it happen with lax rules about lending money. Elizabeth proposed a special department of government designed to keep an eye on lenders and protect borrowers from signing up for risky loans. Elizabeth's idea became a reality with the creation of the Consumer Financial Protection Bureau in 2010.

Elizabeth, her brothers, and her cousins grew up hearing stories about the family's Cherokee heritage: In 1888, Elizabeth's grandmother, Hannie Crawford, drove a wagon into a part of Indian Territory that eventually became Oklahoma. There, she married Harry Reed, whom relatives say was part Native American. Elizabeth's mother was the daughter of Harry and Hannie Reed.

During Elizabeth's campaign to become a senator, her claims of Native American ancestry came into question. In 2012, Elizabeth stated, "Growing up, my mother and my grandparents and my aunts and uncles often talked about our family's Native American heritage. As a kid, I never thought to ask them for documentation—what kid would?—but that doesn't change the fact that it is a part of who I am and a part of my family heritage."

Elizabeth and Jim Warren divorced in 1978. She and Bruce Mann, a fellow law professor, married in 1980. Elizabeth's two children, Amelia and Alex, are now adults with young families of their own; Elizabeth is grandmother to three grandchildren.

Family—her own and those across America—has always been important to Elizabeth. And that's why Elizabeth has made fighting for the middle class—especially middle-class families—her life's work.

BIBLIOGRAPHY

163 Cong. Rec. S850–855 (daily ed. February 6, 2017).

Andrews, Suzanna. "The Woman Who Knew Too Much." *Vanity Fair*, November 2011.

Bierman, Noah. "A Girl Who Soared, But Longed to Belong." *Boston Globe*, February 12, 2012.

———. "An Oklahoma Childhood: US Senate Candidate Elizabeth Warren's Journey from Conservative American Roots." *Boston Globe* video, 7:00. Posted February 12, 2012; www.bostonglobe.com/metro/2012/02/12/for-warren-seeds-activism-forged-plains-oklahoma/rx59B8AcqsZokclyJXkg7I/story.html.

Elizabeth Warren's Senate webpage: www.warren.senate.gov.

G4ViralVideos. "Mitch McConnell Cuts Off Elizabeth Warren's Speech and Has Her Silenced." YouTube video, 2:35. Posted February 8, 2017; www.youtube.com/watch?v=f3IL7oL5oWY.

Griffin, J. Cinder, and Holly Jane Raider. "Women in High School Debate." *Debater's Research Guide: Punishment Paradigms, Pros and Cons*, Wake Forest University, 1989.

Jacobs, Sally. "Warren's Extended Family Split About Heritage." *Boston Globe*, September 16, 2012.

Marquette Nat. Bank v. First of Omaha Svc. Corp., 439 U.S. 299 (1978).

Seelye, Katharine Q. "Warren Says She Told Universities of Her Native American Roots." *The Caucus* (blog), *New York Times*, May 31, 2012, thecaucus.blogs.nytimes.com/2012/05/31/warren-says-she-told-universities-of-her-native-american-roots.

Smiley v. Citibank (South Dakota), N.A., 517 U.S. 735 (1996).

Wang, Amy B. "'Nevertheless, She Persisted' Becomes New Battle Cry After McConnell Silences Elizabeth Warren." *Washington Post*, February 8, 2017.

Warren, Elizabeth. "Sen. McConnell Refuses to Let Sen. Warren Speak About Attorney General Nominee Sessions." YouTube video, 1:07. Posted February 7, 2017; www.youtube.com/watch?v=HVyq6kAN6u4.

———. *A Fighting Chance*. New York: Metropolitan, 2014.

Washington Post. "Sen. Warren Reads Coretta Scott King's Letter About Jeff Sessions Outside the Senate." *Washington Post* video via Facebook/Sen. Elizabeth Warren, 15:29. Posted February 7, 2017; www.washingtonpost.com/video/national/sen-warren-reads-coretta-scott-kings-letter-about-jeff-sessions-outside-the-senate/2017/02/07/2078bc24-edb5-11e6-a100-fdaaf400369a_video.html.

For fighters for fairness everywhere—insist, resist, persist.

—S.W.

To my mom, who fought for me, too.

—S.G.

Cataloging-in-Publication Data has been applied for and may be
obtained from the Library of Congress.

ISBN 978-1-4197-3162-4

Text copyright © 2018 Susan Wood
Illustrations copyright © 2018 Sarah Green
Book design by Pamela Notarantonio

Published in 2018 by Abrams Books for Young Readers, an imprint of
ABRAMS. All rights reserved. No portion of this book may be reproduced,
stored in a retrieval system, or transmitted in any form or by any means,
mechanical, electronic, photocopying, recording, or otherwise, without
written permission from the publisher.

Printed and bound in China
10 9 8 7 6 5 4 3 2 1

Abrams Books for Young Readers are available at special discounts when
purchased in quantity for premiums and promotions as well as fundraising
or educational use. Special editions can also be created to specification. For
details, contact specialsales@abramsbooks.com or the address below.

ABRAMS The Art of Books
195 Broadway, New York, NY 10007
abramsbooks.com